Gumbo Soul

Book of Poetry

Bummi Niyonu Anderson

Printed in the United States of America

ISBN-13: 978-0692401101

ISBN-10: 0692401105

Direction & Editing: Mary Gervin
Cover Design: Femi Anderson
Layout: DoubleXposure Media Group

Life is similar to gumbo. In it, there is love, death, passion, disappointment, and so many other things. All of what we experience— the people we meet, the places we go, the things we do— make us who we are. I am the sum of many ingredients, put together to make a colorful and hopefully delightful dish. Gumbo is similar to life.

For Maya Angelou, Amiri Baraka, and Mary Frances Jenkins

CONTENTS

Writing Recipes

"Writing is an act of faith, not a trick of grammar."

E.B. White

AT 16

Words
were like
water from
a flowing faucet:
Left on unattended,
running over onto
the floors of each room,
deep enough to swim in.
A flood of creative thoughts
unleashed into a mad world
filled with metaphors
and similes, never
quite knowing
where to
go.

WHEN POETS DIE

When poets die, they do so to live again.
Their words are like eternity
Endless and timeless.

When poets die, it is for the ground to yield better fruit
Of what is just,
What is right
And colorful.
Knows no bounds.

When poets die, it is to give birth to other poets
Waiting in the wings.
Listening for the creative voice
To spring forth hope
In a world gone mad.

LOST

Where did you run to?
Did I scare you into a state of darkness
or chase you through thickets of sand spurs?
I look for you,
But it seems I cannot find you.
I call out to you,
But you do not answer.
I wonder where you have gone.
Instead of filling my head with other things,
Maybe I should have cluttered my mind with you.
Now it seems you are lodged beneath
The crazy, the unimportant, and the superficial.
I used to know exactly where you were.
Now the GPS keeps repeating
        "Take the next legal u-turn,"
        then "Recalculating route."
I throw my hands in the air:
Grab the nearest book,
Turn the next page,
Read the next sentence,
Look for the next word
Catapult me to another idea
And into the beginning of
A relevant poem.

NO RHYME WITH REASON

My poems stopped rhyming
When I started living.
No sense in wasting time
When things keep moving.

WRITING
Is
Sensory
Sexual
Sensual
Political
Poetic
Reality
Illusionary
Inspirational
Radically motivating
Intellectually stimulating

All this and so much more...

ALIVE

The sound sends chills up my spine
When I read each word line by line.
I listen in the night hours of my dreams;
Words come flowing into my mind like a stream.
When I stand up among the people to say what is relevant,
I have this strong sense of benevolence.
Words from my heart to my pen have become my voice
Alive, piercing, provoking truth, void of choice.

Flavor of Love

"Where there is love there is life."

Mahatma Gandhi

LOVE

Looking within you
to embrace where love begins
is the truest love.

GODMOTHER

When we talk it feels as if time stands still:
I forget the earth is revolving around the sun,
and since I don't feel it anyway
it makes sense to just enjoy the ride.

I glean from you as a garden.
On any given day
I just might pull up a chair,
sip a glass of lemonade,
face in the sun,
watching you like spring's return.

The return is life for me,
another reason for me to blossom.
I notice something wonderful...
you never left.
I just came to meet you
and the trip has been
worth the wait.

BEAUTY

Beauty needs no words,
Only a semblance of truth.
Defined by each of us,
And who we are
To ourselves.

REMINISCE: A LOVE POEM

The sound of the keys echoes,
Making me take flight into a
Time and space I want to forget.
But I can't ignore the reverberation
Caused by the simple
Massage of his fingers
Across what he loves,
And abruptly
I'm reminded of whom
I once loved.

I stand near him while he plays.
His *Cool Water* scent
Taps me on the shoulder
With a "Hello" and
A "Remember me?"
I am again reminded of
Whom I once loved
And the night of
Discovery.

But then again
Jazz is a silly contrast
Between life and love,
No matter what key
We choose to play in.
The past is best where
It can't be found.

CASINO LOVE

Last night we sat looking out into the Gulf
And a seemingly never ending space.
We laughed hysterically because we
Knew what the other was about to say:
"The casino never closes."
"We can blow all our money and still have each
          other."
You kissed me and wooed every single fiber of my
          being.
My bones weaken with your touch
And the casino lights seemed to dim all along the strip.
We lay together wanting to pierce the innermost parts
          of each other
With romantic interludes tossed between our intense
          lovemaking.
My mind is wrapped around whatever you are
          thinking.
Am I allowed to ponder?
I fell asleep in your arms the moment you kissed me
On my forehead and melted me into liquid form.
You said nothing else,
Even when rowdy winners sounded like
Slot machines gone wild.

ONE SCENE IN A POEM

Robert fell asleep as soon as he sat down on the orange
       couch.
He looked debonair in his pin-striped suit.
Fred Sanford's voice glared in the background from the
       TV.
I laughed when I noticed Robert scratching his beard at
Seemingly the same time as Fred.
I wanted to go over and tickle Robert,
But I knew he'd be ready to fight.
I watched him move and squirm.
He wasn't worried.
I asked him what he dreamed.
He said he dreamed of me.
Generously, I gave him my love,
And now I am empty all
Over again.

MAMA

Roses always bloom
Even when my heart is gloom.
She loves me with all.

BROKEN PIECES

Go and gather you.
Call yourself to every place
You left pieces of you
And gather you.

Go and gather you.
Be it from the mess of your life
Or the cluttered space of others
Call yourself to order
And gather you.

You owe it to yourself
To pick up your life in unwanted places.
And when you're finished,
Put up a sign that reads
"Gone back to me."

FLOODED

My head is flooded with thoughts of you
No life jacket
No preserver.

You won't jump in and save me
And you see me going under.

Would you save me if you knew I loved you?
Give me your hand
Perform mouth to mouth resuscitation
So I can breathe again.

And all those thoughts
Of you
Gush out of me.

I am revived.

FRIENDSHIP

Friendship
Strong, bonded
Endearing, trusting, healing
Stretching beyond normal, loving above fault
Caring, sharpening, comforting
Beautiful, unique
Sibling

GOD'S LOVE

Your love forever,
Finds me in deep dark places.
Saves me from myself

Hardy Stock

"We may encounter many defeats but we must not be defeated."

Maya Angelou

BLACK PEOPLE PLEASE!

(A poetic interpretation of Bishop Victor Powell's words)

Please black people please!
Today is not the day of ease:
You have not arrived.
Don't be fooled by the car you drive.
Come out of your comfort zone;
Stop ignoring the trouble outside your home.
Black kids are dying,
Leaving their fathers and mothers crying.
Where is the desperation for this lost generation?
Do you not know what is going on all around you
Or have you closed your eyes and ears?
Because hearing nothing and seeing
        black will do.

Please, black people, please!
Today is not a day of ease.

SELMA
(For Bob Mants)

It happened just upon a bridge:
People arm in arm,
Dream to dream
Trying to connect with a country
in constant rejection.

What strength of such strong people?
Tear gas couldn't suffocate their collective spirit
Nor deny their time in history.
They returned to the bridge another day
so tomorrow could be mine.

THE DAY YOU LEFT
(For Maya Angelou)

I cried.
I didn't know what else to do.
I prayed.
I had nowhere else to go.
I texted those I love.
I had no one else to understand me.
I rejoiced.
You became an even bigger part of me.
I wrote a poem.
That is what I was born to do.

THE RISE OF THE BLACK MAN

Where is Justice?
Why does it hide its face from the black man?
He looks upon it for light,
But he only gets shade.
No piercing eyes staring with conviction,
Only blinded by its own wayward arrogance.
Justice is.

Where is the black man?
Beating his fists against the bloodied walls of a dream.
People lifting him above irrelevance
And into the light
Of significance.

It is not his blood
But that of a nation who
Knows him not.
He will stand before that nation
And it shall look upon him
And be ashamed.
He will be who he is...
Great he shall be.

I CAN'T BREATHE!

I can't breathe
Because of the pollution
You are spewing
Into the atmosphere.

I can't breathe.
Your political ideology
Yields no fruitful apology,
So I regurgitate your
System of hypocrisy.

I can't breathe.
When you're not choking me,
You strangle my dreams
And leave me gasping for air.

SISTER TO SISTER

I was born to tell you
My sister
That my love for you
Flows like the waters of the Nile
And what life and spirit that comes from me
Is for you and the gifts
You have given to the world.

You are as the full moon,
Giving light in deep darkness.
When life is without form and void,
You come like the Spirit of God
Saying "Let there be light."
You are Ruth, Naomi, and Mary.
You are my sister.

You are the hope that God's blessings have given.
Your sweet and gentle nature is the scaffold
That shall become the peace of the earth.
You are my Africa in America,
            Beautiful and strong
You are Nefertiti, Cleopatra, and the Queen of Sheba.
You are my sister.

You are the first history book
        Speaking to the greatness of the struggle
        Of the slave and free.
        A queen before the captivity.
Despite the rugged path and dark night,
You are like the North Star
        guiding us into what we can become.
You are Harriet, Sojourner, and Fannie Lou.
You are my sister.

You are the architect of the greatest survival,
The painter whose brush creates a joy unspeakable
        into the hearts of our people.
Every stroke is a symbol of justice,
Every word is a vessel of freedom.
You are Maya, Sonia, and Nikki.
You are my sister.

You breathe your spirit into me and
I rejoice from the depths of my soul.
Africa is embedded in your very nature
And she comes into existence
        through your nurture and grace.
You are a symbol of my heritage,
        A star that guides.
You are Angela, Bernice, and Betty.

You are my sister.

You are the mother of the earth
        The mother of Jesus,
            Of Moses and Muhammad.
An African queen you are.
I know you
        I know myself.
You are a woman
        Beautiful
        Black

I am...

LIBERTY

Shackles hide liberty's reality
As men fight with strong vitality.
It is with noble observation
That liberty is as invocation.
Where there is a cause
Let us find no reason to pause.

BLACK IS BEAUTIFUL

I am as beautiful as the sunrise over the Atlantic.
Everything about me is an awesome wonder,
For I am beautiful.
Even my thoughts are like precious crystal
So I hold them carefully and treat them with
        meticulous attention.
My thoughts are beautiful.

My every feature is the essence of beauty.
I don't look down on myself
I know He made me this way.
My nose may be big but it's who I am,
As I am large in my countenance.
Men look at me in wonder.
How come she's so beautiful?

I am many shades, I am my own rainbow.
I am tan, brown, vanilla, and chocolate.
All of which are so beautiful even I have learned
To shake my head in amazement at my own self.
Look at me, I am many dimensions
That even when I walk, eyes turn and feet stand still
They stop and wonder what it's like to be me.

You look at my lips and say they're too big
Yet you want them as your own,
Because they seem to do more than speak.
The fullness of my lips makes even a simple kiss
        worthwhile.
Men forget their names
While sistahs sing.

I have been raped by the words of others
        and told to hate myself,
But something inside me keeps telling
Me...
I...am...stunning!
My hair comes in many textures,
That none can keep their hands out of it.
Whether it is the kinkiness or the waves,
It makes the hair stand up on your head!
I make you ask questions only I can answer
That you're still scratching your head when I'm
        through.
Even you have realized
I AM BEAUTIFUL!

BLACK IS LEGACY

I am from the very loins of Kings made slaves,
Brought from the shores of Africa in chains.
Not knowing what was ahead only what remained.
I am inside them...from generation to generation.
I am their legacy.

Who knows my yesterday better than those before me?
I listen as they speak of such great pain yet
Inside them lies such great faith
And strength to overcome anything.
I am their legacy.

Between the pages of what history failed to say
I find truth of who I really am
And write the stories that should be told.
I am bound to lives that survived all storms,
Even those whose names are unknown.
I bring what they are to who I am.
I am their legacy.

Let me always remember when I should be a fool,
Not to shame so great a people when second-class
        stood for me.
Even when I was yet unknown to the world they

   hoped a better day for me.
I am their legacy.

Who am I?
I am Harriet Tubman—I challenge your fears.
I am W.E.B. Dubois—I inspire your intellect.
I am Marcus Garvey—I remind you of Africa.
I am Phyllis Wheatley—I let my words become yours.
I am a story no one can deny nor bury in the sand.
I am their legacy.

I am a reminder.
Even before America,
I am.

BLACK IS AFRICA

Quick! Open your ears!
Listen...do you hear what I hear?
The sound flows across the Atlantic into my living
        space
And seeps through my very bloodline into every place,
Even where I am yet to occupy.
I am Africa and
Africa is me.

Come now and open your eyes!
I want you to see the real Africa and not the lies.
There is no Tarzan swinging from tree to tree,
But a land rich with great destiny.
I hold the world in my very hands,
Don't you be the last to know.
You are Africa.
Africa is you.

Reach out to me as I am a part of who you are.
I still long for you no matter how far.
I gave you to the rest of the world my beloved one
So when you return you'd be as the sun,
Having risen above all the pains of history
Into something so wonderful and glorious.

You have done much with little.
You are African.

Men have worked to keep you from knowing me.
Men have done so, so you wouldn't know of your
          royalty.
You are from the first kings and queens that ever
          reigned,
Dominion flows through your very veins.
All that is beautiful is from you sweet Africa,
You are the window into my soul.

The soil of your earth has infused into who I am, Africa!
Your name means, "Pleasant."
Is this why others drill in search of you?
For they have not known pleasant until they find you.

Africa, in all of us.

BLACK IS CREATIVE

We are like a master-skilled potter
We take pain and turn it into promise
Like clay we mold our minds with imagination
And dream our way out of despair.

Is there a sound we have not heard deep within us
Or a canvas waiting to receive what is etched in our
         memory?
We dance in the face of adversity and find pearls
         beneath obstacles
Like no other man our pain feeds us like fatted cows.
We become what our dreams dare.

Take us uptown and we play the Savoy and the Cotton
         Club.
Men of all colors want to see what makes the piano
         keys dance.
My fingers represent where I've been and where I'm
         going,
I make no distinction.
I just play till the sun comes up and
I haven't even touched heaven yet.

Watch my feet as they glide across the stage.

Look closely you'll see my confidence is impeccable.

My mind is already miles ahead.

I try to teach others to dance even when the sky is gray

But they keep waiting for blue skies.

Me, I just dance myself into a weather change and leave you in wonder.

BLACK IS KINETIC

Look out below!
I'm here with a little rhythm and a little rhyme,
So bad I can turn one cent into a dime!
You don't believe me, just watch my feet
As I rhyme to the sound of the beat.
I scat with my tongue and rap fluid and free.
I am as kinetic as they come if you just let me be.
I am poetry in motion with a tap gone crazy mad
And if you put me in these shoes I'm so good I'm bad.
I put to rhythm what another might put to words
I bring to life creativity that has yet occurred.
Watch me now...

BROTHAS & SISTAHS

Brotha,
be
better
being,
not banging.
Battles
are
won
with
the
ballot
not
the
bullet.

Listen!
Look!
Let
love's
light
lift
you.

Sistah,
sing
songs.
Smooth
sounds,
symbolic
of
names
that
are
yours.

Listen!
Look!
Let
love's
light
lift
you.

Together,
time
touches
tempers
and

cools
consciousness.
Wrap
each
other
in
one
another
and
let
love's
light
lift
us.

ABOUT MR. BALDWIN

His words are like fire
Touching them you will get burned
But live to ask why.

FREE
(Acrostic Poem)

Facing every obstacle unimaginable
Reality of not seeing tomorrow
Every slave Harriet got to leave
Entered the space of possibilities.

WARRIORS
(For Charles Sherrod)

Standing on the shoulders of men,
We dare not sit unless to bend
And listen as the elders speak
To ensure future days not bleak.

Standing on the shoulders of women,
Not to repeat history again
But their lessons we humbly keep
To ensure future days not bleak

Elders, we call out to you first
Since you have seen the days of thirst.
It is your knowledge that we seek
To ensure future days not bleak.

Warriors, cast your spears into our hands!
Where you fought, your legacy stands:
Our fight for justice, strong not weak
To ensure future days not bleak.

NIGGAS BE
(Before I Buried the N-Word)

Niggas be knowin' bout the brothas
When the brothas come around
Clown around
      Git down
      Fool around.

Niggas be knowin' bout the sistahs
'Round the way
Teasin' day to day
      Gittin' no play
      Got much to say.

Niggas be knowin' the rap
Brothas wearing their colors cap
Sistahs gettin' slapped
But niggas don't know shit 'bout the Revolution!

NIKKI

Hey Nikki
With your gold shining hair-fro.
What it is?
What it be?
You are all that and
A book of poems!

"Auntie" Nikki,
I got a word or two from you
Maybe three
Live
Laugh
Love
Write a poem for me.

Reading you
Like making love under the moon
Until the sun rises
Or a protest march
To keep the Dream alive
And to love
Malcolm
By any means necessary.

I see you
A free spirit
A guiding light
Smooth caramel skin
As Hip as can be

Black, beautiful, and free.
Free to think,
Write,
And kick ass.

Right on!
Dig it!
I'm ego tripping.

I HEARD A BLACK MAN SAY

Strong willed as my father would be,
I began to look inside me.
Look at the few chances I am given,
As I pursue the life I'm living.
I am Black.
To some it's still not enough,
But understand that to live a life
Fulfilling is hard and rough.
I am a man,
One made to understand
Your plights and mine.
They say I'll soon fail
They say I'll wind up in jail.
They say my development is late
They say I'll drop out of school before I graduate.
They say though I'm not a slave,
I'll wind up in an early grave.
I am the Black male.
I've been handed the anchor
Before I get the chance to set sail.
But I will rise from where I have been
Tho' you think I'm a lost cause, you will see me win.

In the Mix

"Nothing is pleasant that is not spiced with variety."

Francis Bacon

UNWANTED GUEST

I never call before I make my entrance
Even if you know months in advance
My visit is still unexpected.
No one can pin down the exact second
          of my visitation.
My timing is never perfect, but sure.
Sometimes I come to get the sick and suffering.
My arrival may be sweetness to the one I come to see
          But leave a bitter taste in the mouths of those who are left.
If I stay too long, my presence leaves
          a distinguishable stench.

Why do I exert my power over the powerful and the
          powerless?
The strongest man falls to his knees and balls himself
          in a corner when he sees me.
He beats his fist against the hardwood floor beneath
          him.
Weakened by my indelible presence that shrank his
          heart into that of a little boy.
I make grown men cry.
I fill their hearts with anger and
A million questions I don't even turn to answer.

My sting is as a wasp disturbed innocently
        by two kids falling against marigolds.
You don't always know I'm there
Until I've gone in for the kill.
You disturb my peace with your dangerous living,
No regard for youth and
A belief you will live forever.
You eat what you shouldn't eat
Then never think to exercise
Until your doctor tells you I'm making
        reservations.

I never stay around to comfort the wounded
And the faint of heart knows I don't come to make
        friends.
No apologies utter from my lips—
If you're waiting for me to say I'm sorry, I won't.

Even if the sun is shining,
Its radiance is overtaken by a deep, dark depression
And smothered by the dimness I bring.
I never come to stay.
I guess that's why I never make friends.

QUESTIONS

When I want to ask certain questions,
        my words retreat into a shell.
My thoughts become wayward and
        so flustered that I cannot tell.

Sadly, it's really not the questions at all,
        but the insecurities I feel that make me small.
Even a giant who loses himself in fear
        will inevitably shrink.
It's the mind that knows.

DREAMS

Where do dreams go when the dreamer leaves?
Is there a place in heaven where they sleep
or do they steady the world with inferred realities?
Can dreams live longer than the dreamer
or are they buried with men who conceive them?

Dreams never sleep.
They give place to other dreams
so the dreamer lives.

LIVE FROM MAMA'S BELLY

How can I see inside the womb?
I don't know if I have enough room
       To move
       To be
       To create
All I know, it is dark in here
       No light
       No sight
       No switch to flicker with
Just darkness and me
Looking at one another;
Wanting light to rescue one from the other.

EXCUSES

I could
and I should
but I won't
and
I don't know why
or why not.

Maybe
Maybe not
Perhaps
I look side-eyed
Never knowing what to expect

A simple yes
Or no will do.

DADDY

Hands of this man big,
I knew not one hiding place
But his protection.

MENTORS

When they speak you live.
You find yourself thinking more
Than yesterday's thoughts.

ALBANY

The good life city
Is home sweet home no matter
Winter spring or fall

WINTER

The trees know no sway
They stand staring in patience
Waiting for spring's dance.

WHEN SEASONS CHANGE

The fall of summer
Brings instant joy to my heart.
Leaves bow in respect.

IMAGINE

I know you see me
Making moves
And leaving you
Going head first into
Indescribable places and
New realities that leave you
Envious of what you could have had.

I SEE YOU

I see you staring.
I make your pretenses fall
And you just wonder.

TWINS

From the womb, the two of us
Still sharing the same space
With brushes, paper, ink, and pen
Ensuring that art will never end.

SOMETHING GREATER

Even if you get to know me,
You will never know all of me.
I keep
Growing
Evolving
Transforming

I'm just too much for one lifetime,
Too big for one stratosphere.
Every time I try to shrink,
I burst out into something greater than before.

NO WORDS

Hazelnut accentuates an already crowded place
The sun attempts to beam through her hollow space
Too bright to shine upon her face
She wears sunglasses to watch you plead your case.

She enters as laughter and gossip fill the room
As noon day news is nestled between noise and gloom
Of seeing you sitting waiting with roses in full bloom.
Little do you know of the news that looms.

Every single inch of her hurts
Blackened and blued even more as you blurt
Out you love her and it sickens her that your flirt
Is a sad and manipulative attempt to divert.

You telling her you're sorry is simply not enough.
Stroking her does not make it tough
To leave since the same hand handled her rough
When it balled up and punched her with rebuff.

Silence has become her mode of fear
All because you chose to force her near
And now the surrounding laughter you no longer hear
When her sunglasses hide bruised eyes full of tears.

TEACHERS

Like a strong wind
Blowing
Pushing us into places
Growing
Never too far to reach us
Knowing
Close enough to give more
Sowing
Treasures always a part of us
Glowing